Contents

 **Fall**

Spring

Winter

Anytime

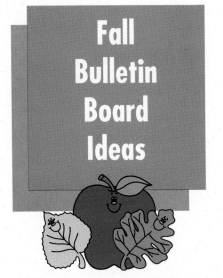

Fall Bulletin Board Ideas

Perfect for welcoming fall, this bulletin board also serves as a colorful display of student work. Use orange paper to cover the board. Enlarge and color the **bushel basket pattern** (page 115), personalize it with your name, and mount the basket in the center of the bulletin board. Use red, yellow, and green paper to duplicate the enlarged **apple pattern** (page 102). Write each student's name on an apple pattern and display the apples along with samples of student work on the board.

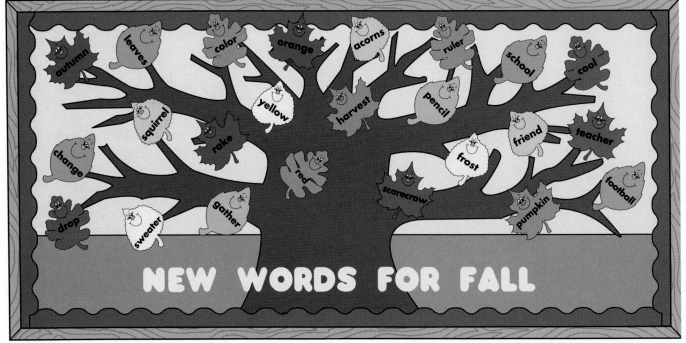

Celebrate fall—and learning—with this seasonal display. Cover the bulletin board with sky blue paper along the top and add green paper across the bottom to create a horizon line. Use brown paper to create a tree, then mount it onto the bulletin board. Make several copies of the **leaf patterns** (pages 52 and 55) and allow students to color the leaves with fall colors. Write spelling words or unit vocabulary words on the leaves and mount them on the tree's branches.

Collecting reading "nuts" is easy with this autumn bulletin board. Cover your bulletin board with yellow paper, then enlarge and color the **squirrel pattern** (page 101). Make several copies of the **acorn pattern** (page 102) and **leaf patterns** (pages 52 and 55), then have students color and cut them out. Label the acorn patterns with autumn book titles and place them on the bulletin board. Have students label the leaves with their names, then place the patterns next to their favorite books.

Greet your students on the first day of school with this colorful school tools display. Cover your bulletin board with white paper and mount an enlargement of the **backpack pattern** (page 103) in the center of the board. Personalize the backpack with your name and grade level. Make several copies of each of the **school tool patterns** (pages 100 and 114). Write each student's name on a school tool pattern and then mount the patterns on the bulletin board.

Fall

Give the students in your class a "sweet" welcome with this delicious bulletin board display. Cover your bulletin board with yellow paper. Enlarge and color the **mixing bowl pattern** (page 117) and personalize the mixing bowl with your name and grade level. Copy a **cookie pattern** (page 117) for each child in your class. Then, write each student's name on a cookie pattern and mount the patterns around the mixing bowl. To create a colorful border, make several copies of the **oven mitt pattern** (page 113). Color the patterns using a variety of markers or crayons. Display the patterns around the outside of the bulletin board. If desired, trace the oven mitt pattern on several scraps of wallpaper, then cut out the patterns and display along the bulletin board border.

Your students will get a kick out of this spirited display. Use light green paper to cover your bulletin board and mount an enlarged **football player pattern** (page 126). Enlarge the **football pattern** (page 121) and personalize the pattern with your name and grade level. Attach the pattern to the bulletin board. Then, duplicate and personalize a small football pattern for each child to mount on the board. Accentuate the display using real pom-poms or create your own using colored tissue paper. If desired, use school colors to decorate the display.

You're sure to create bright smiles with this display. Cover your bulletin board with white paper. Enlarge the **crayon pattern** (page 56) to make a large crayon and personalize the crayon with your name and grade level. Mount the large crayon on one side of the board and add a matching construction paper "scribble." Copy a class supply of smaller crayon patterns. Have the students color the crayon patterns using a variety of colors. Personalize the smaller patterns with the students' names and mount the small crayons on the board.

Your students will get the "point" that you're happy to meet them with this colorful, fun display. Cover the bulletin board with light blue paper. Enlarge the **apples with chalkboard pattern** (page 51) and attach it to the center of the board. Add a welcome message. Duplicate a class supply of the **pencil pattern** (page 100) and personalize each pattern with the name of a student. Complete the display by attaching the pencils around the welcome artwork.

Fall

Make your students "wise" to the achievements of others with this seasonal bulletin board. Cover the board with royal blue paper and use green paper to create a horizon line. Mount a tree made of brown paper along one side of the board. Enlarge the **owl pattern** (page 123) and mount the owl on one of the tree's branches. Make copies of the **leaf patterns** (pages 52 and 55) in fall colors, and write the name of each student on a leaf. Attach student work to the display, and add the personalized leaves to the papers.

Your students are sure to enjoy comparing birthdays with this colorful display. Cover the board with orange paper, then make enlargements of the **fall boy** and **fall girl patterns** (page 65). Mount the boy and girl on opposite sides of the board. Make several enlargements of each **balloon pattern** (pages 74, 105, and 121) so that you have a total of 12 balloons. On each pattern, write the name of a month and the names of students whose birthdays fall within that month. Mount the balloons on the board.

COLOR US HELPFUL!

Attendance ✓ Jamal
Lunch Count ✓ Jack
Calendar Sherri
Papers Susan
Tables Lori
Chalkboard Jeff
Homework Erin

Doors ✓ Shirley
Bookshelves ✓ Tim
Mail Kevin
Library Spencer
Computer Justin
Recycling Tanya
Lights Lucky

Color your classroom with this job assignment board. Use white paper to cover the bulletin board. Enlarge the **crayon box pattern** (page 102) and mount the pattern on one side of the board. Use brightly colored crayons to write classroom jobs. Duplicate and personalize a **crayon pattern** (page 56) for each student. Affix a hook-and-loop fastener to the back of each crayon pattern. Draw checkmarks on the bulletin board with colored chalk or cut out checkmarks from colored posterboard. Reassigning tasks is as easy as taking down one student crayon and replacing it with another.

WELCOME!

Vince, Ling May, Victor, Christy, Jordan, Brandon, Perez, Spencer, Edward, Kate, Rachel, Ray, Pam, Tyrone, Lea, Mandy, Lynn, Shirley, Eden, Penny, Janet, Gene, Phillip, Erica, Steve, Patti, Dawn, Sherri, Lynette, Peter

A GREAT PLACE TO HANG YOUR HAT

Your students will take their hats off to this creative welcome board. Cover the board with light blue paper. Duplicate a class set of the **hat pattern** (page 107). Write the names of your students on the hats and mount them on the bulletin board. Later, the hats can be used in a job assignment board, to choose leaders for class activities, or to assign groups or teams.

Let your students know they are the "apples of your eye" from the very first day of school with this inviting bulletin board. Cover the board with sky blue paper and add additional sheets of green paper to create a horizon line across the bottom. Enlarge the **schoolhouse pattern** (page 55) and place it in the center of the board. Add enlarged copies of the **sun pattern** (page 56) and the **flag patterns** (pages 57 and 121) to accent the school yard. (Flags of both the United States and Canada are provided.) Then, make a class set of the **apple pattern** (page 102) and personalize each apple with a student's name. Complete the school yard scene by mounting the apples on the bulletin board.

"Crow" about your students' work with this display. Cover the bulletin board with light green paper and mount an enlargement of the **scarecrow pattern** (page 118) in the center. Then, surround the scarecrow with enlarged copies of the **haystack pattern** (page 117). Attach student work to the haystacks and accent each haystack with a **crow pattern** (page 119). Add visual interest by cutting an irregularly shaped background to highlight the title of the board.

Your students can pick a peck of ideas with this display. Cover the background with sky blue paper and create a horizon line by adding several sheets of green paper. Use brown paper to construct a tree for the center of the board. Copy and enlarge the **fall boy pattern** (page 65) and the **bushel basket pattern** (page 115) and attach them to one side. Enlarge the **leaf** (pages 52 and 55) and **apple** (page 102) **patterns** onto appropriately colored paper and allow students to write topic ideas on the patterns. Arrange the leaves and apples on the tree, and add a friendly **squirrel pattern** (page 101).

Provide "plenty" of praise and recognize good student work with this bulletin board. Cover the board with yellow paper. Make an enlargement of the **cornucopia pattern** (page 124) and mount on one side. Make several copies of the **apple** (page 102), **corn** (page 53), **acorn** (page 102), **pumpkin** (page 119) and **banana** (page 118) **patterns**. Place construction paper in fall colors behind student papers, attach to the board, and accent with the fruits, nuts, and vegetables. Complete the display with an additional row of food patterns across the bottom border.

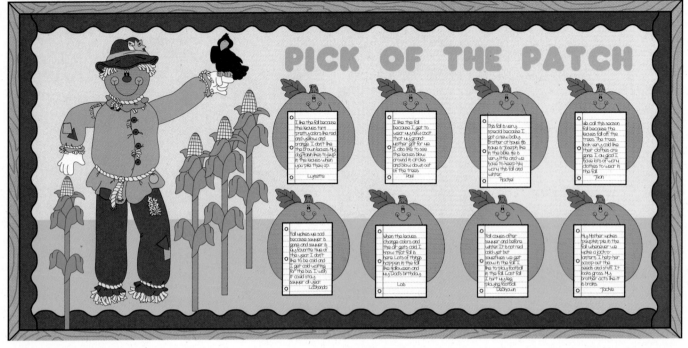

Post perfect papers in this pumpkin patch. Cover the bulletin board with light blue paper and add green paper along the bottom to create a horizon line. Enlarge the **scarecrow pattern** (page 118) and mount the scarecrow on one side of the board. Surround the scarecrow with enlargements of the **cornstalk pattern** (page 54). Create a pumpkin patch by attaching enlargements of the **pumpkin pattern** (page 119) to the board and add exceptional student papers.

This appealing bulletin board will highlight your students' favorite books. Use light blue paper to cover the bulletin board. Enlarge the **apple pattern** (page 102) and mount the apple in the center of the board. Make several copies of the enlarged **apple core pattern** (page 102), and ask students to name their favorite books. Write the titles on the apple cores and attach to the board. If desired, the class may vote on favorites or each student may be given her own pattern on which to write her favorite book title.

10

"Ears" looking at outstanding work on this bulletin board. After covering the background with bright green paper, enlarge and mount a **bear pattern** (page 59) in the center of the board. Enlargements of the **cornstalk pattern** (page 54) should be added to the sides of the display. Mount student work on the board. Highlight each paper with an enlarged copy of the **corn pattern** (page 53).

Add a "whoosh" of fun and color to your classroom with this bulletin board. Cover the board with sky blue paper and add green paper along the bottom to create a horizon line. Enlarge the **sliding dog pattern** (page 58) and attach it to the board. Add an enlarged **sun pattern** (page 56) to the sky. Make a safe place for the sliding dog to "fall" by adding copies of the **leaf patterns** (pages 52 and 55) on the "ground" of the board. For added interest, combine the leaf patterns with real leaves the students have collected.

11

Celebrate a "beary" happy Halloween by adding this bulletin board to your school. Use orange paper to cover the board. Then enlarge the **cowboy bear** (page 50) and the **tooth fairy bear** (page 49) **patterns** and attach the bears to opposite sides of the display. Make enlargements of the **pumpkin pattern** (page 119) in varying sizes and mount the pumpkins in the center of the board. Add several copies of the **bat pattern** (page 59) to complete the board.

Tempt your trick-or-treaters with this fun Halloween display. Cover the board with purple paper. Enlarge the **cowgirl pattern** (page 52) and the **boy in a tiger suit pattern** (page 54) and mount the boy and girl patterns on opposite sides of the board. Make enlargements of varying sizes of the **ghost pattern** (page 53) and attach the ghosts around the center of the display.

Teach good values with this Thanksgiving bulletin board. Using light green paper, cover the board. Enlarge the **turkey pattern** (page 122) and mount it in the center of the display. Make enlargements of the **feather pattern** (page 107). Write the name of a value on each feather and mount the feathers to make the turkey's tail on the board. Make several copies of the **leaf patterns** (pages 52 and 55) and **acorn patterns** (page 102). Use the leaves and acorns to add interest to the bottom border of the display.

Your students will be thankful for a chance to share their Thanksgiving thoughts on this display. Begin by covering the board with light blue paper. Then enlarge the **Pilgrim bear** (page 124) and the **cornucopia** (page 124) **patterns** and mount on either side of the bulletin board. Make a copy of the **pumpkin pattern** (page 119) for each of your students and allow them to write what they are thankful for on their pumpkin. Mount the pumpkins on the board, and use several copies of the **leaf patterns** (pages 52 and 55) as accents.

Winter Bulletin Board Ideas

Use this display to encourage students to get cozy with books. Cover the background of the board with blue paper. Enlarge the **bedtime bear pattern** (page 104) and place it in the center of the board. Make a blanket out of construction paper, a towel, or a fabric piece and mount it on the bulletin board. Add several copies of the **snowflake pattern** (page 105) with book titles on them to complete the scene.

Use these penguins to showcase outstanding work. Cover the board with sky blue paper. Create a winter landscape with white paper placed along the bottom half of the board. Use enlargements of the **snowy tree pattern** (page 108) to make a forest. Line up several enlargements of the **penguin pattern** (page 107) along the bottom of the board. Mount student work in each penguin's upraised "hand." Finish by adding a **sun pattern** (page 56) to the sky area of the display.

Let your students know you appreciate the "gift" of their hard work with this display. Cover the board with yellow paper. Make enlargements of both the **elf bear pattern** (page 64) and the **Santa bear pattern** (page 63) and mount them on opposite sides of the board. Make a class set of the **gift pattern** (page 92) and write a student's name on each gift. Add the gifts to the board.

There's a winter wonderland of wonderful work on this display. Cover the board with light blue paper. Attach student work to colorful construction paper and mount on the bulletin board. Make several copies each of the **snowman** (page 123), **snowflake** (page 105), **mitten** (page 126), **snowy tree** (page 108), **penguin** (page 107), and **winter kids** (page 106) patterns and use the patterns as accents for the student papers.

Winter

Use this bulletin board to "snow" off student excellence. Cover the board with blue paper. Add white paper along the bottom of the board to create a snowy landscape. Enlarge the **snowman pattern** (page 123) and place it in the center of the display. Post student work and accent each paper with a copy of the **snowflake pattern** (page 105). Write students' names on the snowflakes, and use other snowflakes as additional decorations for the board.

Students will be eager to get a good book in their hands when you add this display to your classroom. Cover the board with white paper. Make several enlarged copies of the **book pattern** (page 114). Write book titles on the patterns, or allow students to write the titles of their favorite books on the patterns. Mount the book patterns on the bulletin board, and use several copies of the **mitten pattern** (page 126) to add a warm touch to the arrangement.

Bring the fun indoors with this wintery display. Cover the board with blue paper, then add white paper to create a rolling horizon line of snow drifts. Enlarge the **winter kids patterns** (page 106) and place them on opposite sides of the board. Make several copies of the **snowflake pattern** (page 105) and arrange these in the "sky" as though it is snowing in the scene.

This bulletin board is a great way to get students "fired up" about reading. Use yellow paper to cover the board. Make an enlargement of the **fireplace pattern** (page 61) and place it in the center of the display. Make several copies of the enlarged **book pattern** (page 114) and add titles to each book using black marker. Mount the books to the board. Accent each book and the fireplace itself with copies of the **stocking pattern** (page 60).

Winter

Add a heavenly touch to your classroom with this display! Use light blue paper to cover the board. Make a class set of the enlarged **bear angel pattern** (page 112) and add students' names to each bear. Mount the bears on the board. Make the board three dimensional by creating clouds with cotton balls and attaching the clouds to the board.

Celebrate the holiday work of your "elves" with this Christmas bulletin board. Cover the display with yellow paper. Mount student work on seasonally-colored construction paper and then attach the papers to the board. Copy a **Santa pattern** (page 110) for each student and write the students' names on the patterns. Accent each student paper with the appropriate personalized Santa pattern.

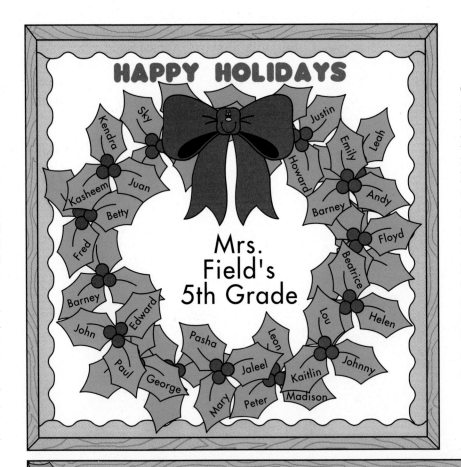

Get into the "holly"-day spirit with this seasonal display. Use white paper to cover the board. Then make several copies of the **holly cluster pattern** (page 108). Write the name of each of your students on a leaf of holly. Use the holly clusters to form a wreath shape on the bulletin board. Be careful not to overlap or cover up a student's name. Add the finishing touch with an enlargement of the **bow pattern** (page 109) placed at the top of the wreath. If desired, each student could be given a holly cluster and asked to write his name on one leaf. On the other leaves he might write one thing he hopes to receive during the holidays and one thing he hopes to give to another person during the season.

Shine a little "light" on your star students with this holiday bulletin board. Begin by covering the board with dark blue paper. Mount student papers to the board. Top each paper with an enlargement of the **flame pattern** (page 66), and place an enlargement of the **candle holder base pattern** (page 66) below each student paper to create a "candle." Add enlargements of the **bow pattern** (page 109) to the board, and place an enlargement of the **holly cluster pattern** (page 108) in each corner of the board for a final touch.

19   © Carson-Dellosa Publ. CD-0094

Winter

Celebrate the holiday season with this "tree"-rrific display. Cover the board with light blue paper. Mount an enlargement of the **snowy tree pattern** (page 108) in the center of the board. Make enough copies of the **ornament pattern** (page 58) for each of your students. For a three-dimensional effect, add yarn or ribbon tied in a bow to the top of each ornament. Allow students to write their names on the ornaments and attach them to the board.

Use this bulletin board to share "tasty" books with your students. Use white paper to cover the background of the display. Create a cookie tree by mounting copies of the **gingerbread man pattern** (page 53) on the board in a tree shape. Write the title of a book on each gingerbread man. Create a base for the "tree" with brown construction paper. Finish the bulletin board with copies of the **holly cluster pattern** (page 108) placed in each corner of the board.

These reindeer bring more than Santa's sleigh—they also bring examples of outstanding student effort. Use blue paper to cover the background of the board. Enlarge the **reindeer pattern** (page 62) and place the enlargement in the top center of the board. Attach student work to the display, and highlight each piece of work with a smaller copy of the reindeer pattern. Add a snowy accent with copies of the **snowflake pattern** (page 104) in various sizes.

Light up the Hanukkah season with this menorah bulletin board. Use dark blue paper to cover the background. Enlarge the **menorah pattern** (page 111) and place in the center of the display. Add enlargements of the **candle pattern** (page 109) to the branches of the menorah. Mount enlarged copies of the **dreidel pattern** (page 80) on light-colored construction paper and place them in the bottom corners of the bulletin board. For an added activity, remove the flames from the candles and mount only the candlesticks on the menorah. As each day of Hanukkah passes, have a student "light" the menorah by adding another flame.

Winter

Kwanzaa comes alive with this display. Use white paper to cover the board. Enlarge the **kinara pattern** (page 98) and mount it in the center of the board. Attach copies of the **kinara candle pattern** (page 98) to each candle holder of the kinara. Complete the board by adding a row of fruits and vegetables below the kinara, including copies of the **corn** (page 53), **pumpkin** (page 119), and **apple** (page 102) **patterns** as well as items from the **cornucopia pattern** (page 124).

Let your students "chime in" with their New Year's hopes on this bulletin board. Cover the board with white paper. Make an enlargement of the **bell pattern** (page 90) and personalize it with your name and grade level. Attach the bell to an upper portion of the display. Make a class set of smaller copies of the bell pattern. Allow each student to write his hopes for the New Year on his bell. Have students add their names to the bottom of their bells. Mount the bells on the board.

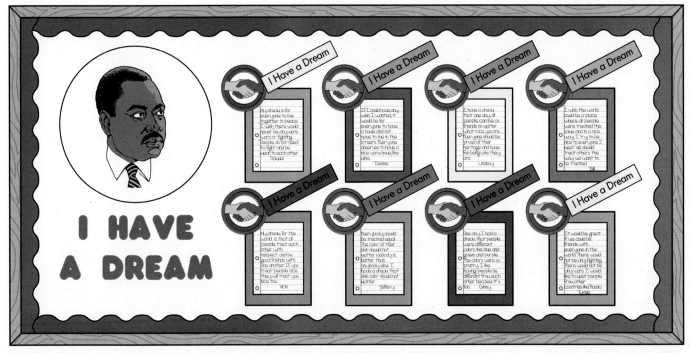

Celebrate the birth of Martin Luther King, Jr., with this bulletin board. Use white paper to cover the board. Enlarge the **Martin Luther King, Jr., face pattern** (page 60) and place it the top left corner of the board. Allow students to compose papers about their dreams, and mount their work on construction paper attached to the board. Accent each paper with a copy of the **handshake circle pattern** (page 122) and strips of construction paper on which you have written the phrase "I Have a Dream."

Introduce students to another culture with this colorful bulletin board. Begin by covering the board with light blue paper. Make an enlargement of the **Chinese dragon pattern** (page 111) and mount the dragon in the center of the board. Duplicate a class set of the enlarged **fortune cookie pattern** (page 119) and add a student's names to each cookie. Arrange the fortune cookies around the dragon to complete the display.

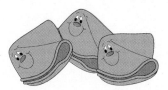

Winter

Don't hide student work "underground;" display it on this bulletin board. Use sky blue paper as a background for the board. Add green paper along the bottom of the board to create a horizon line. Enlarge the **sun pattern** (page 56), and place the sun in the sky area of the board. Enlarge the **groundhog pattern** (page 96) and place the groundhog so that he appears to be rising up out of the ground area of the board. Attach student work to the display. Add a realistic touch by creating shadows from black paper.

Valentine's Day will be "purr"fect when you place this display in your classroom. Begin by covering the board with light blue paper. Enlarge the **valentine cat pattern** (page 69) and personalize it with your name and grade level. Mount the cat in the top center of the board. Then, make a class set of the valentine cat patterns and add students' names to the patterns. Attach the smaller valentine cats to the board.

Students will fall in love with reading when they see this bulletin board. Cover the board with pink paper. Write the titles of books on enlargements of the **book pattern** (page 114) and mount them to the board. Allow students to write their names on copies of the **valentine heart pattern** (page 66). Students can then attach their hearts to the titles of their favorite books or the books they are reading.

Let this bear steal your heart as she helps you celebrate Valentine's Day in your classroom. Begin the display by using white paper to cover the board. Make an enlargement of the **heart bear pattern** (page 68) and mount it on one side of the board. Attach an enlargement of the **bushel basket pattern** (page 115) to the opposite side of the board. Fill the basket and surrounding area with copies of the **valentine heart pattern** (page 66) personalized with the names of your students. Add a final touch with a copy of the **bow pattern** (page 109) mounted to the bushel basket.

Spring Bulletin Board Ideas

"Spring" this display on your students. Use sky blue paper to cover the board and place green paper along the bottom to create a grassy area. Enlarge and personalize the **flower pattern** (page 127), then mount the pattern in the center of the board. Personalize a class set of the **small sunflower pattern** (page 128) with students' names and mount the patterns in the grassy area. Add a finishing touch by adding copies of the **sun pattern** (page 56) and **butterfly patterns** (pages 62 and 128) to the display.

Your students will "bug out" when they see this scene filled with grinning insects. Begin the bulletin board by covering the background with sky blue paper. Use green paper to create a horizon line. Enlarge the **sunflower pattern** (page 99), and place several of these sunflowers in the "grass" of the display. Add multiple copies of the **bug patterns** (page 70), the **butterfly patterns** (pages 62 and 128) and the **bee pattern** (page 115) to complete this bug lover's dream.

Smiles will "sprout" when you add this colorful display to your classroom. Use blue paper to cover the board and add bright green paper along the bottom to create a horizon line. Enlarge the **sun pattern** (page 56) and place it in the sky portion of the board. Make enough copies of the **sunflower pattern** (page 99) for each of your students. Write the students' names on the flowers and mount the flowers on the display. As a finishing touch, add copies of the **butterfly pattern** (page 62) in the corners of the board.

You'll create quite a "buzz" with this cheerful bulletin board. Start by covering the board with light blue paper. Enlarge the **beehive pattern** (page 113) and mount the bee hive in the center of the display. Add your name and grade level at the bottom of the board. Make a class set of enlarged **bee patterns** (page 115) and personalize each with the name of a student. Complete the scene by attaching the bees to the board. If desired, use spelling or unit vocabulary words instead of student names to create a study board.

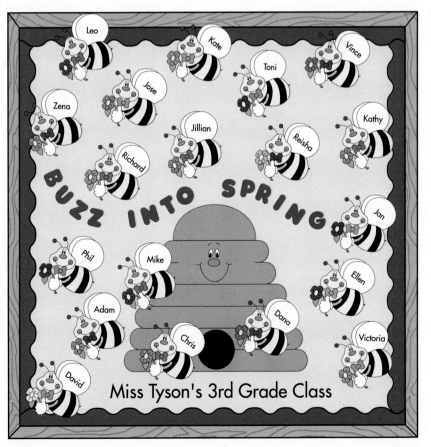

Spring

Celebrate the sweet smell of student success with this display. Begin by covering the board with yellow paper. Choose student papers to mount on construction paper in springtime colors. Attach the papers to the board. Accent each paper with a copy of the **sunflower pattern** (page 99) and the enlarged **skunk pattern** (page 71).

Encourage good "bee"havior with this bulletin board. Cover the background with sky blue paper. Then, add green paper along the bottom of the board. Add several strips of green scalloped bulletin board border to the garden to create the illusion of garden rows. Make several copies of the **small sunflower pattern** (page 128) and "plant" them in the garden. Make a class set of enlarged **bee patterns** (page 115) and personalize each with the name of a student. Reward good student behavior by mounting students' bees on the display.

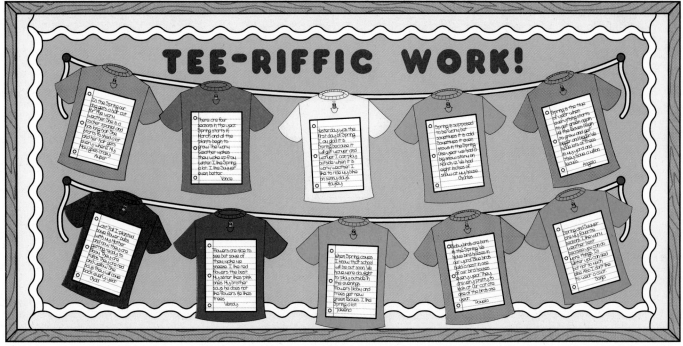

Dress up your bulletin board with this playful display. Enlarge several copies of the **tee shirt pattern** (page 57) on brightly colored paper. Mount a student paper on each tee shirt. String a clothesline or other cord to the board to create a three-dimensional effect. Then, add the tee shirts to the clothesline. For added interest, attach the tee shirts to the clothesline using real clothespins.

Somewhere over the rainbow there's a treasure of outstanding student work. Celebrate student achievement with this eye-catching display! Cover the board with light blue paper. Then, enlarge the **pot of gold pattern** (page 73) and mount the pot near the center of the board. Create a rainbow by adding strips of colored paper. Attach student papers to the board, and accent each paper with a copy of the **gold coin pattern** (page 52) personalized with a student name. Complete the display with a border of the gold coin pattern.

Observe St. Patrick's Day with this colorful and charming display. Cover the board with white paper. Enlarge the **St. Patrick's Day bear pattern** (page 72) and mount the bear in the center of the board. Place enlargements of the **shamrock** (page 74) and the **pot of gold** (page 73) **patterns** on either side of the bear. Scatter copies of the gold **coin pattern** (page 52) and the shamrock pattern across the board.

Irish (and even non-Irish) eyes will be smiling when they see this holiday display. Cover the bulletin board with sky blue paper. Enlarge the **pot of gold pattern** (page 73) and place it in the lower center of the board. Add copies of the **St. Patrick's Day bear pattern** (page 72) on either side of the pot. Make a class set of the **gold coin pattern** (page 52), personalize each coin with a student's name, and arrange the coins on the display. A border of the **shamrock pattern** (page 74) lends a finished look.

Encourage students to share their efforts and emerge from their "cocoons" with this colorful display of great student work. Use light blue paper to create a sky. Mount student papers on the bulletin board. Accent each student paper with an enlargement of the **butterfly pattern** (page 128). Add visual interest to the board by adding clouds made from cotton balls.

Great student work comes in many "colors of the rainbow;" let your students know that their efforts are worthwhile with this bulletin board. Begin by covering the board with light blue paper. Create a rainbow using colored paper or markers. Mount student papers above the rainbow. Add large clouds at either end of the rainbow with cotton balls. Make additional clouds along the top of the bulletin board by adding cotton balls.

Spring

Encourage "brilliance" with this unique bulletin board. Cover the background with alternating wedges of yellow and orange paper. These wedges will form the sun's rays in the finished display. You may wish to use gold foil wrapping paper, if available. Enlarge a copy of the **sun pattern** (page 56) and mount it in the center of the board. Arrange student papers in a circle around the sun to complete the display.

Students will "catch" on to the idea of helping in the classroom with this display. Cover the board with light blue paper. Add strips of green paper for grass. Enlarge the **baseball boy pattern** (page 98) and mount him on one side of the board. Write job assignments on enlarged **baseball glove patterns** (page 58) and mount the baseball gloves on the board. Make a class set of enlargements of the **baseball pattern** (page 71) and personalize each with a student's name. Place a baseball in each baseball glove to make job assignments. Complete the display with a baseball border across the bottom.

Celebrate the return to warm temperatures and sunny days with this joyful bulletin board. Cover the board with light blue paper and add green paper to create a horizon line. Make a large tree using brown and green paper. Enlarge the **swinging cat pattern** (page 86) and place it on the board. Mount copies of the **flower** (pages 79), **bug** (page 70), **sunflower** (page 99), **butterfly** (page115) and **bee** (pages 62 and 128) **patterns** to add life to the scene. Tuck an enlargement of the **sun pattern** (page 56) behind the tree as a final touch.

Cultivate pride in achievement with this garden-themed bulletin board. Begin by covering the board with blue paper. Add green paper to the bottom of the board to create a garden area. Add rows to the garden with strips of green scalloped bulletin board border. Enlarge the **gardening girl pattern** (page 81) and mount the girl to one side of the board. Enlarge the **sun** (page 56) and the **flower** (page 79) **patterns**. Place the sun in the "sky" and "plant" the flowers in the garden. Attach student work to the display. To complete the display, add several copies of the **butterfly pattern** (page 62).

Spring

Great writing takes "root" on this flowery display. Cover the bulletin board with white paper. Enlarge the **flowerpot pattern** (page 83) several times and mount the enlargements to the board. Add a selected piece of outstanding student work to each flowerpot.

Welcoming spring is a breeze with this attractive display. Use sky blue paper to create the background. Enlarge a class set of the **hot air balloon pattern** (page 67) and personalize each balloon with a student's name. Mount the balloons on the board. Add three-dimensional clouds fashioned from cotton balls.

34

Celebrate spring-time fun with this bulletin board. Cover the board with blue paper. Add green paper to the bottom of the board to make a horizon line. Enlarge the **girl bear** (page 95) and **boy bear** (page 97) **patterns** and mount them on the bulletin board. Attach enlarged copies of the **kite pattern** (page 92) and add colored yarn for a three-dimensional effect. Add enlarged copies of the **flower pattern** (page 79) along the bottom of the bulletin board and in the background. To complete the display, mount copies of the **ladybug** (page 70) and **butterfly** (page 128) patterns on the bulletin board.

Get all your ducks in a row with this seasonal display. Cover the board with blue paper. Add green paper to the bottom of the board to make a horizon line. Enlarge the **rain girl pattern** (page 81) and place the girl in the middle of the board. Create a rain cloud with white paper, and add a spring shower with the **raindrop pattern** (page 115). Make a class set of the **duck pattern** (page 79) and personalize the ducks with the names of your students. Mount the ducks on the board.

Spring 🐝

It's "raining" interesting reading on this bulletin board. Cover the background with light blue paper. Enlarge the **book pattern** (page 114) and write the title of an appropriate book on each pattern. If desired, allow students to supply the names of their favorite books. Make a class set of enlarged **umbrella pattern** (page 86) and personalize them with students' names. Allow students to place their umbrellas next to the books they are reading or their favorite books. For a final touch, "sprinkle" copies of the **raindrop pattern** (page 115) over the display.

This is one "rain shower" you'll love! Use light blue paper to cover the board. Make enlargements of the **rain bear** (page 77) and the **flower umbrella** (page 76) **patterns** and mount them on either side of the display. Create rain with copies of the **raindrop pattern** (page 115). Complete the board with copies of the **flower** (page 79) and **sunflower** (page 99) **patterns**.

36

"Crack" open a "carton" of good work with this Easter display. Cover the board with lavender paper. Add green paper and cut and feather the edges to create grass. Enlarge the **girl bunny** (page 82) and **boy bunny** (page 85) **patterns** and mount on either side of the board. Enlarge a class set of the **egg pattern** (page 53) and personalize each egg with a student name. Mount student papers on the display, and accent each with a personalized egg. Add a creative border of eggs using pastel paper.

This many-colored bulletin board brings a international flair to your classroom. Cover the board in green paper. Make an enlargement of the **Cinco de Mayo hacienda pattern** (page 109) and attach it near the top of the display. Add enlargements of the other **Cinco de Mayo patterns** (page 109) to the board. Complete the display with an enlargements of the **Mexican Big Kids patterns** (page 91).

37

Anytime Bulletin Board Ideas

WHAT A SHARP CLASS!

This "sharp" bulletin board is a great way to showcase student work any time of the year. Cover the board with orange paper. Attach student papers to colored construction paper and mount on the board. Make several enlargements of the **pencil pattern** (page 75) and use the pencils as accents for the student work.

LIGHT THE WORLD WITH A SMILE!

Mrs. Wilson's 3rd Grade

Asa · Jana · Benji · Kurt · Carrie · Dion · Lisa · Erica · Marc · Fran · Gary · Helen · Ian · Susan · Rollie · Quisha · Pam · Nina · Opal

You're sure to create cheery smiles with this "toothsome" display. Use bright blue paper to cover the background. Make an enlargement of the **tooth pattern** (page 90) and mount in the top center of the board. For additional visual interest, allow a portion of the tooth to overlap the border of the bulletin board. Then, make a class set of the tooth pattern. Personalize the teeth with the names of your students. Mount the personalized teeth on the board.

WE "GOPHER" GOOD BOOKS

It will be easy to encourage your class to "gopher" new books with this bulletin board. Begin by covering the board with yellow paper. Center an enlargement of the **gopher pattern** (page 78) on the board. Write the titles of books on enlarged copies of the **book pattern** (page 114) and mount the books around the gopher.

Students will learn the rules of good behavior in no "time" with this bulletin board. Cover the board in light blue paper. Make enlargements of the **watch pattern** (page 89). Write a classroom rule for good behavior on each watch, and mount the watches on the board. To create a unique border, use additional copies of the watch pattern with hands drawn in around the edges of the board.

WATCHING OUR BEHAVIOR

39

Anytime

Your students will be "feline" great when they see their outstanding work displayed on this creative bulletin board. Cover the board with light blue paper. Enlarge the **cat pattern** (page 89) and mount it on the board. Attach selected student work to colorful pieces of construction paper and mount these papers on the board.

Students will be ready to sink their teeth into reading when you add this display to your classroom. Cover the board with light green paper. Then, enlarge the **dog pattern** (page 113) and mount the dogs on one side of the board. Mount several enlarged **book patterns** (page 114) and write the titles of books on the patterns, and attach the books to the board. Make a class set of the enlarged **bone pattern** (page 127) and personalize each bone with a student's name. Allow students to place their bones next to the title of the book of their choice. Add a border using copies of the bone pattern.

Organize your classroom with this "handy" display. Start by covering the board with white paper. On large pieces of construction paper, write the various tasks that must be done in your classroom and mount the jobs on the board. Then, make a class set of the **hand pattern** (page 128) and write students' names on the hands. Assign jobs by placing a student hand next to the name of the task she is assigned.

Books take on a fresh "sparkle" with this striking bulletin board. Use dark blue or black background paper to make the colors of the board stand out. Then, add enlargements of the **ring pattern** (page 126) on which you have written the titles of books. If desired, allow students to provide the names of their favorite books. Create a sparkle for each ring with white chalk.

41

Anytime

Students will flock to "check" out each other's good work when they see this inventive bulletin board. Begin by creating a checkerboard effect by attaching black and red paper squares to the board. Mount student work on the display, and use enlargements of the **checker pattern** (page 122), personalized with student names, to accent each piece of work.

No one can resist a freshly popped batch of popcorn! Orange paper forms the background of this bulletin board. Add an enlargement of the **popcorn popper pattern** (page 88) to the center of the board. Make enlarged copies of the **popcorn kernel pattern** (page 88) for the class and personalize the patterns with the student names. Mount the kernels to the board to complete the display.

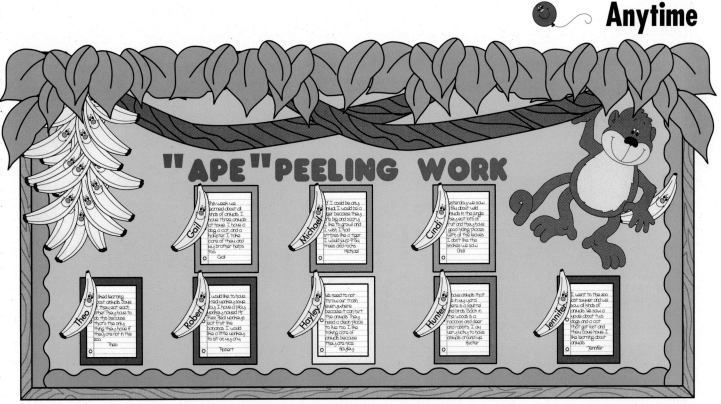

Highlight the efforts of your students with this bulletin board. Cover the board with bright green paper. Create a vine with rolled brown craft paper or paper bags. Enlarge the **monkey pattern** (page 116) and place it on one side of the board. Create a bunch of bananas with copies of the **banana pattern** (page 118) and mount it on the other side of the board. Affix student papers to colored paper, accent each with a copy of the banana pattern, and attach the work to the board. Add a canopy made from copies of the **leaf pattern** (page 105) attached to the top of the board.

Your students will "flip" for this display. Cover the board with light blue paper. Add tree branches made from brown paper. Attach enlargements of the **opossum pattern** (page 114) to the branches of the "tree." Mount copies of student work on the board and write the name of each student on the opossum pattern.

Anytime

Encourage your students to soar to new heights with this bulletin board. Cover the board with sky blue paper and add clouds made of cotton balls for a three-dimensional touch. Enlarge the **airplane pattern** (page 120), personalize the pattern with your name, and mount the airplane in an upper corner of the board. Attach student work to construction paper and add to the display. Accent each paper with a personalized copy of the airplane pattern.

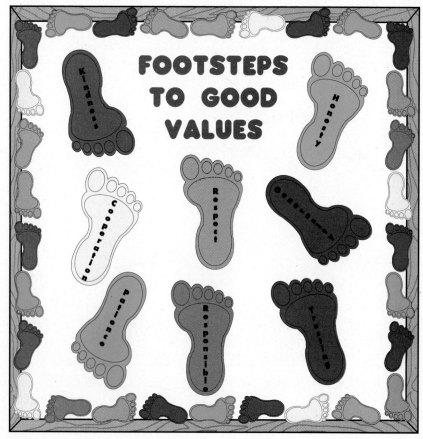

Help your students take the first "step" toward good values with this colorful display. Create a background using white paper. Make enlargements of the **footprint pattern** (page 92) and write the name of a value on each. Mount the footprint patterns to the board. Add a finishing touch with a border made from copies of the footprint pattern.

All the world loves a clown, and so will your students! Cover the board with yellow paper. Mount an enlargement of the **clown pattern** (page 120) in the center of the board. Make a class set of the **balloon patterns** (pages 51, 74, 105, and 121) on brightly colored paper, and personalize each balloon with students' names. Attach the balloons to the board above the clown's head. Add a whimsical touch by creating balloon strings from colored yarn or string.

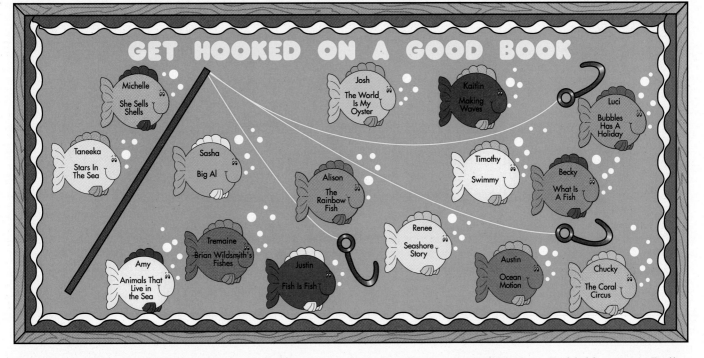

Get your students "hooked" on reading with this underwater scene. Cover your bulletin board with blue paper. Roll a piece of brown paper into a thin tube to represent a fishing pole, then add yarn for fishing line. Make several copies of the **fish** (page 100) and **hook** (page 100) **patterns,** or for a three-dimensional effect, fashion hooks from aluminum foil. Place the hook patterns at the ends of the yarn. As each student reads a book, give him a fish pattern to color, label with the title of his book, and cut out. Place the completed fish on the board.

Anytime

You'll be able to show off more than a "pocketful" of good student work when you add this bulletin board to your classroom. Cover the board with yellow paper. Make an enlargement of the **overalls pattern** (page 80) and attach it to one side of the board. Personalize an enlargement of the **pocket pattern** (page 80) with your name, and mount the pocket in the upper corner of the display. Write the bulletin board title on posterboard and place it in the large pocket. Make additional copies of the pocket pattern and add student names to the small pockets. Attach the small pockets to the bulletin board, and slip student work into the pockets. You may need to enlarge the pocket patterns to fit the size of your students' papers.

"Sing" the praises of your students with this bulletin board. Use yellow paper to create a background. Enlarge the **music sheet pattern** (page 93), add your name and grade level with black marker, and mount the music sheet pattern in an upper corner of the board. Attach student work to colorful construction paper and add the work to the display. Accent each student paper with a copy of the **music note pattern** (page 77).

Stress the importance of good manners with this "sweet" bulletin board. Cover the board with white paper. Enlarge a copy of the **ice cream cone pattern** (page 116) and write your name on the pattern with black marker. Mount the ice cream cone in an upper corner of the display. Make slightly smaller enlargements of the ice cream cone pattern and write a rule for good manners on each cone. Attach these smaller cones to the board. Finish the bulletin board by adding a border of copies of the ice cream cone pattern.

Students will need eight arms to carry all the good books they'll find on this bulletin board. Use light blue paper to create a watery background. Enlarge the **octopus pattern** (page 94) and attach the octopus to the center of the board. Write the titles of books on enlarged copies of the **book pattern** (page 114). If desired, allow students to supply the titles of their favorite books. Mount each book on an arm of the octopus. Multiple copies of the **fish pattern** (page 100) complete the marine scene.

47

Anytime

"Color" your students' world "read" with this display. Begin by covering the board with white paper. Enlarge the **artist octopus pattern** (page 87) and mount it on the board. Add book titles to enlarged copies of the **book pattern** (page 114) and attach the books to the board. Complete the scene by drawing "paint splatters" with markers or cutting the splatters shapes from construction paper.

An elephant never forgets to reward exceptional student effort; reward your achievers with this "bright" board. Begin by covering the board with orange paper. Then, mount an enlargement of the **elephant pattern** (page 84) to one side of the board. Attach student papers to the board, and accent each with a personalized copy of the **light bulb pattern** (page 93). Create a colorful burst behind the word "bright" in the bulletin board's title with construction paper.

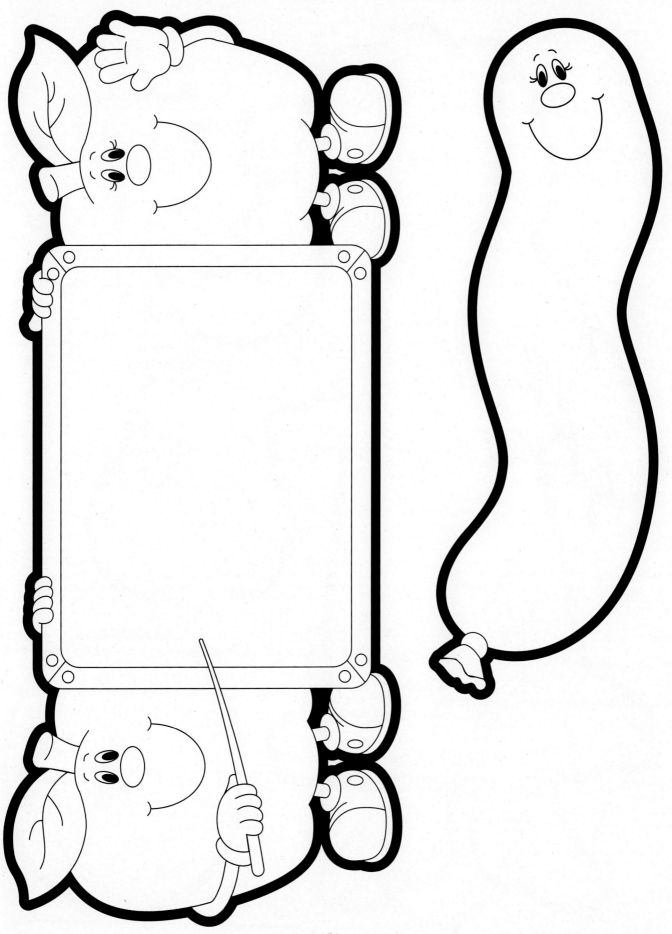

51

53

54

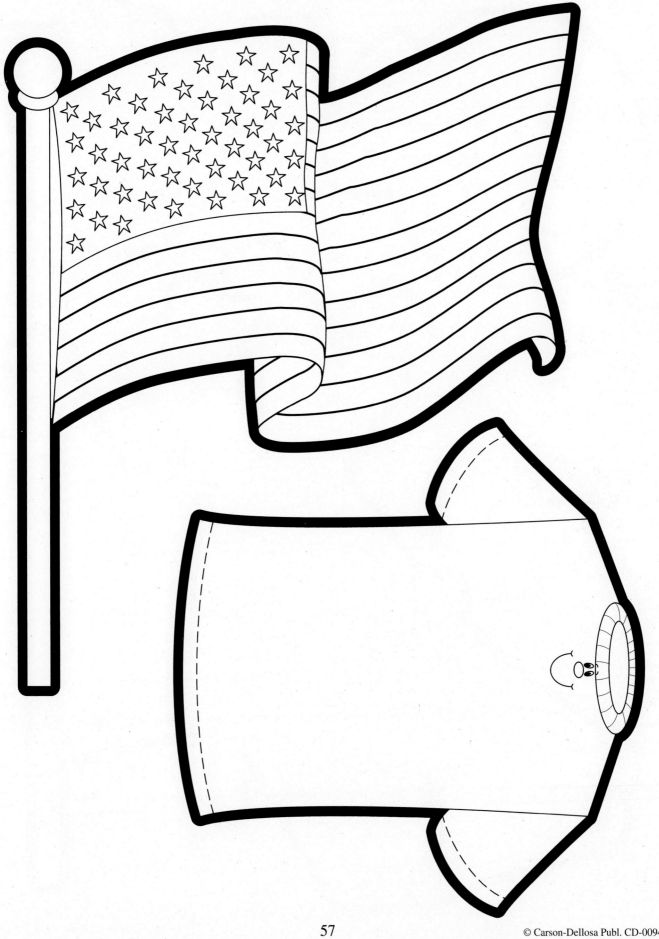

58

60

61

62

65

66

67

68

71

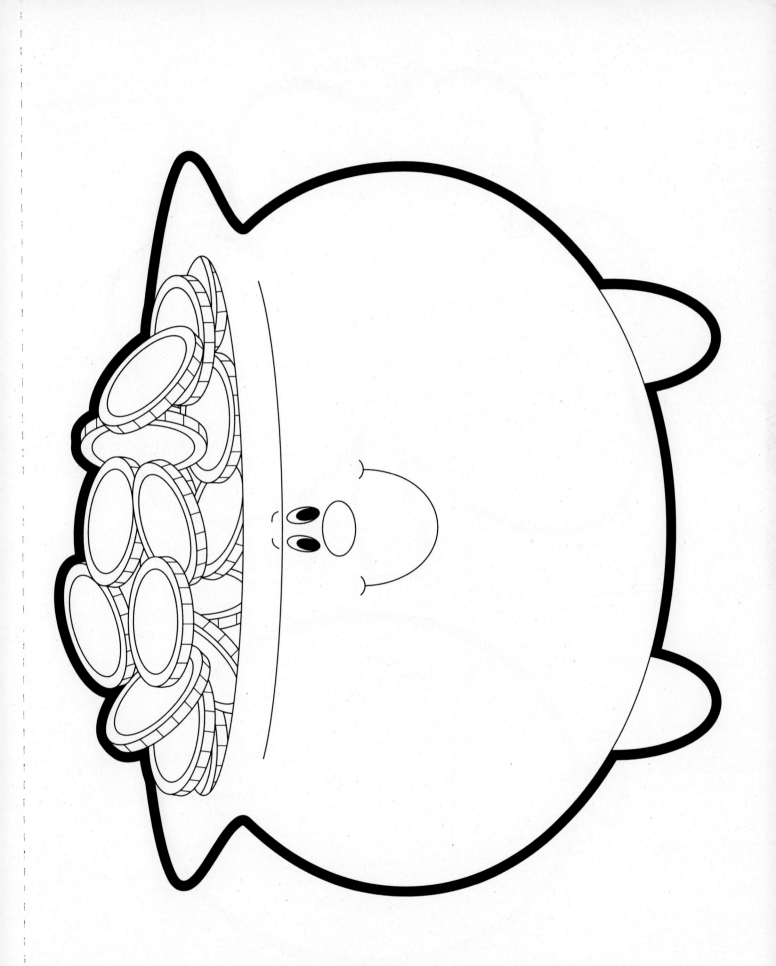

73

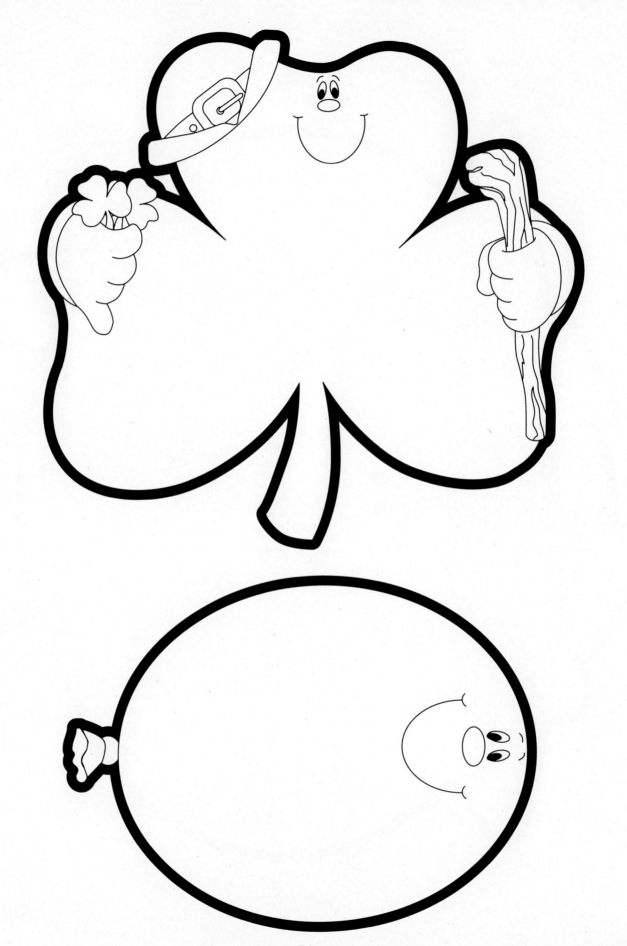

74

75

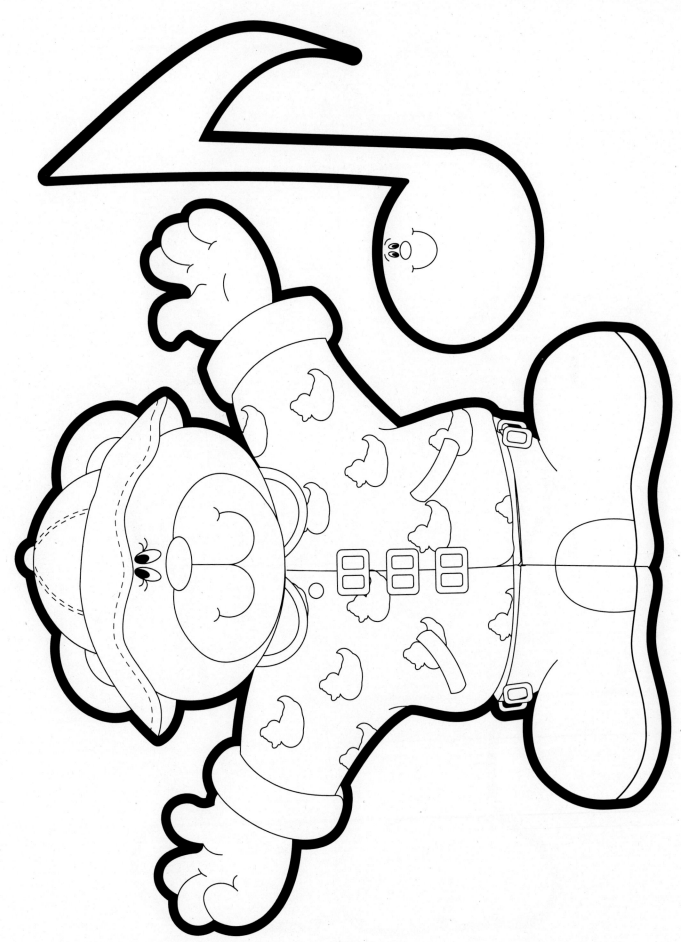

79

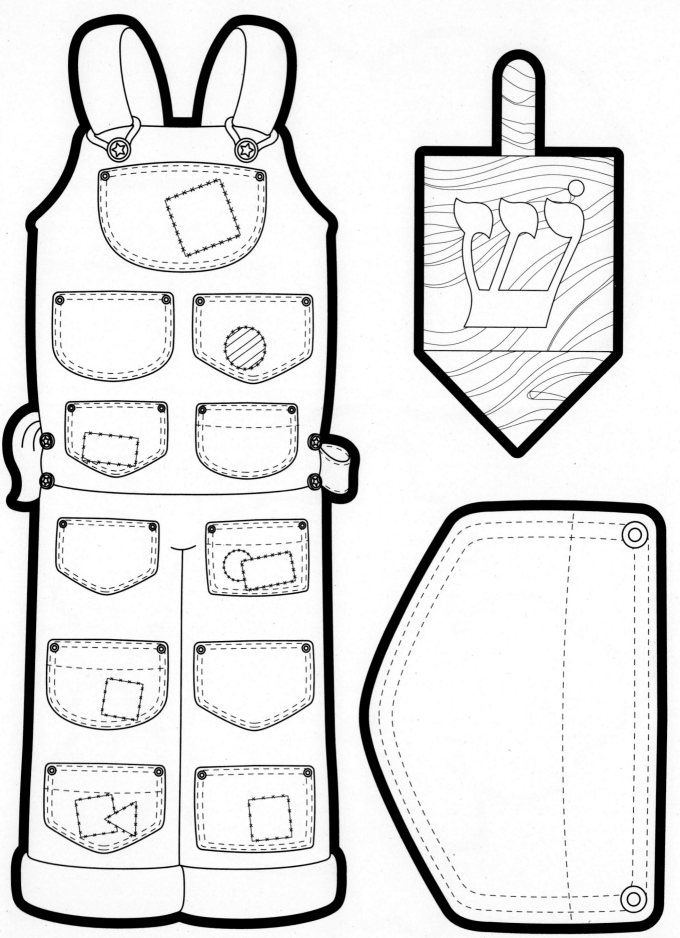

80

81

82

85

Blue

Red

88

89

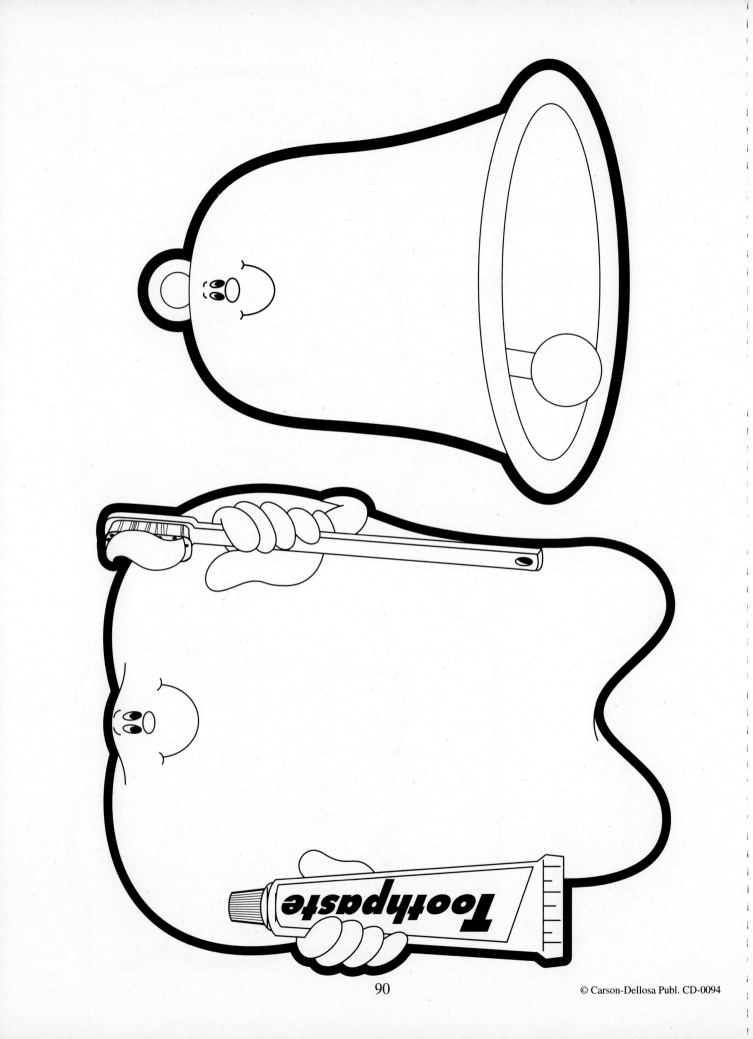

90

91

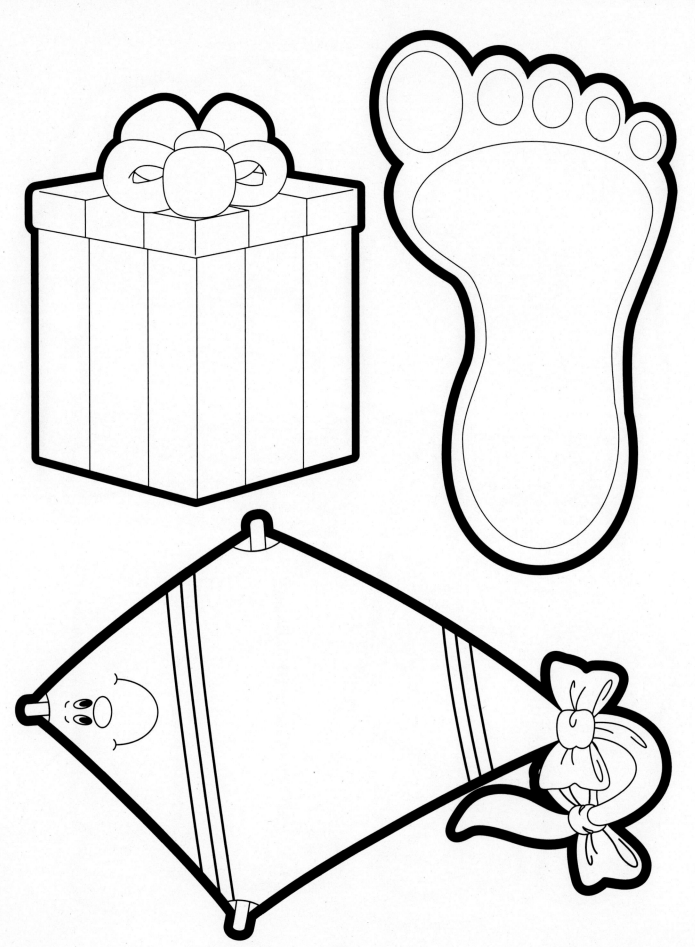

94

95

100

101

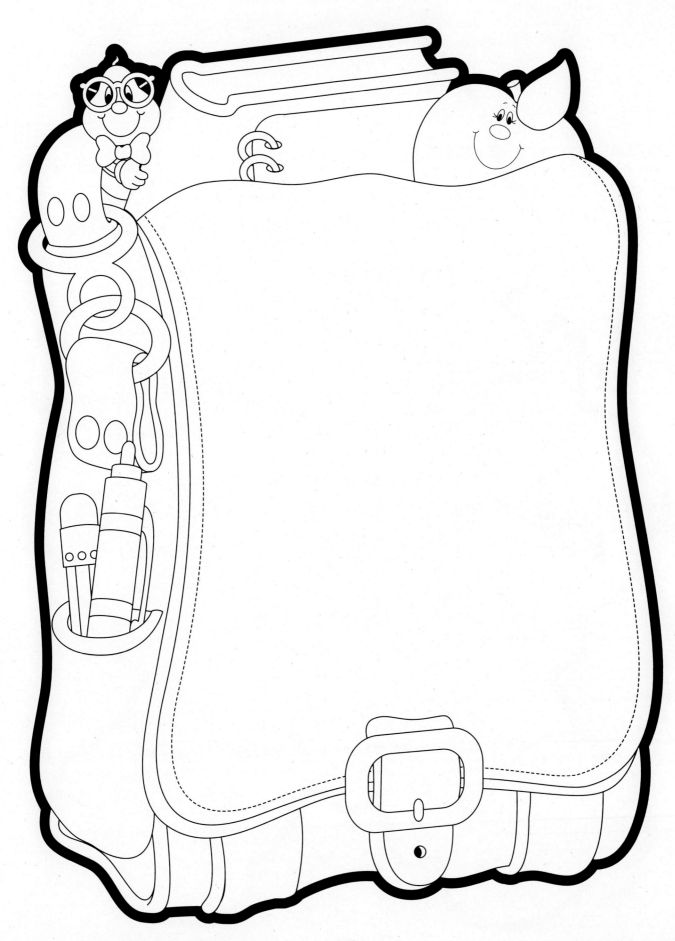

103

104

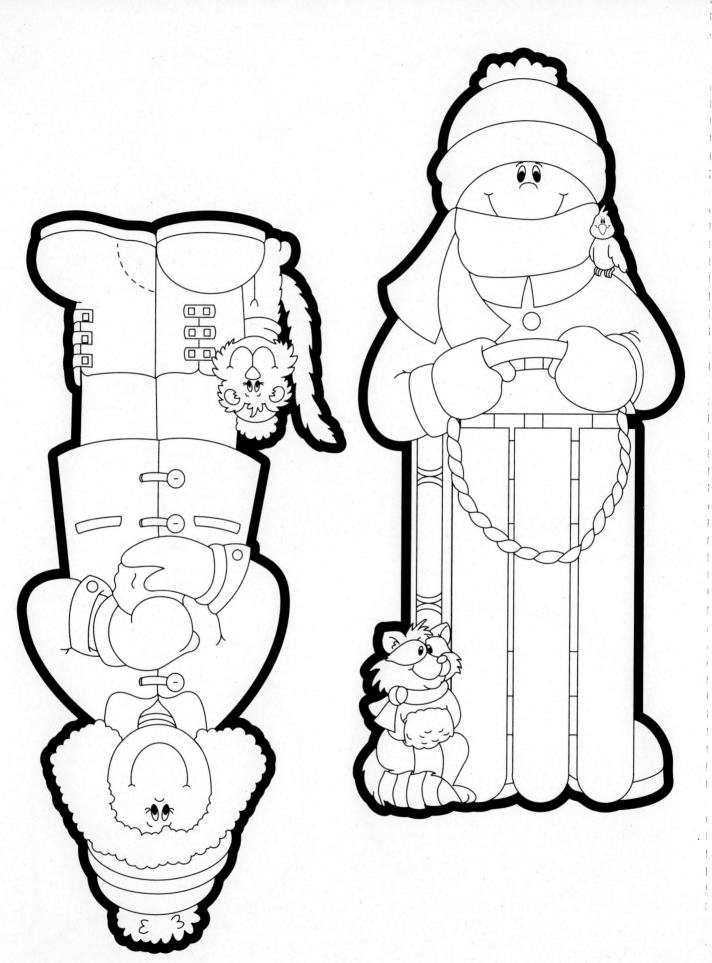

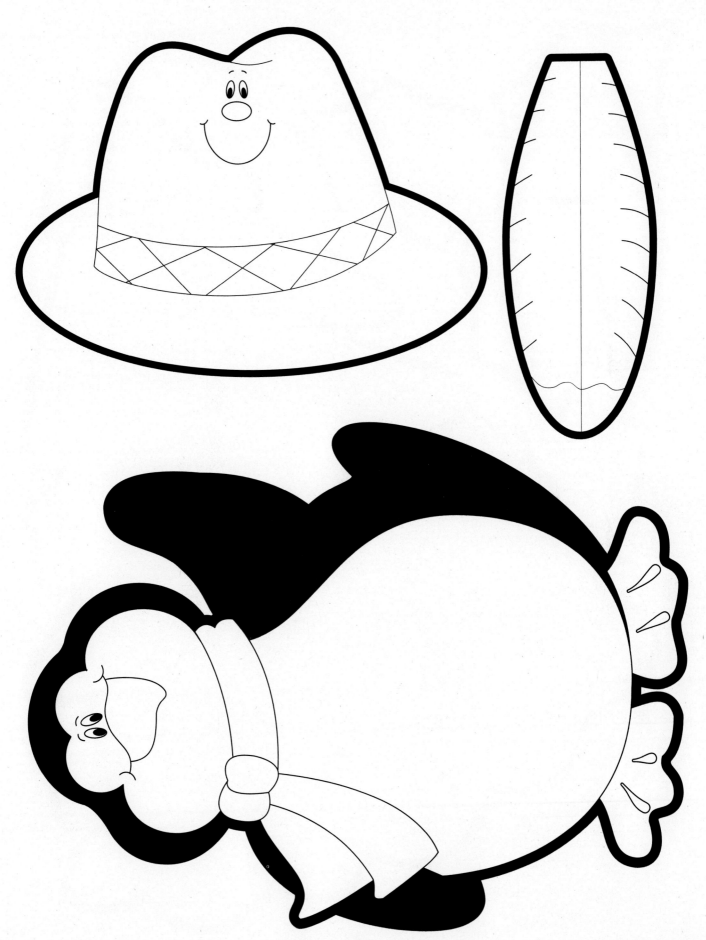

108

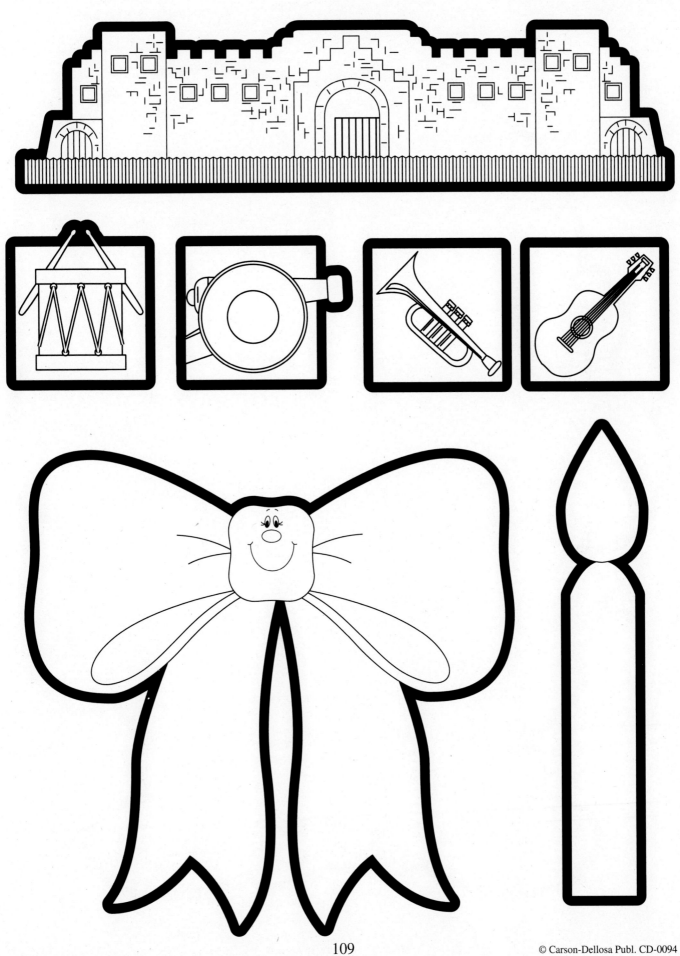

110

112

113

114

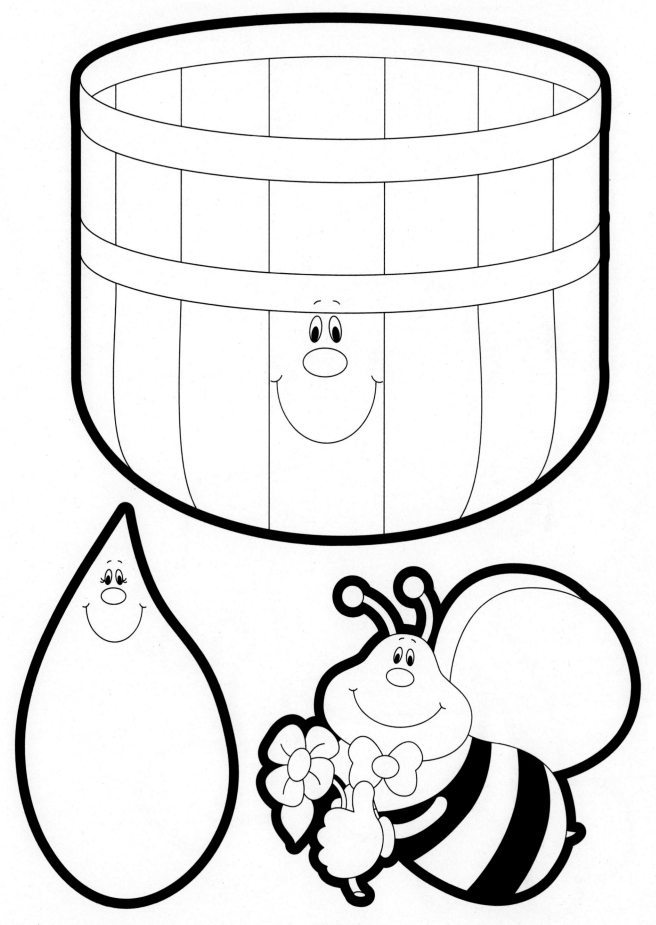

116

118

119

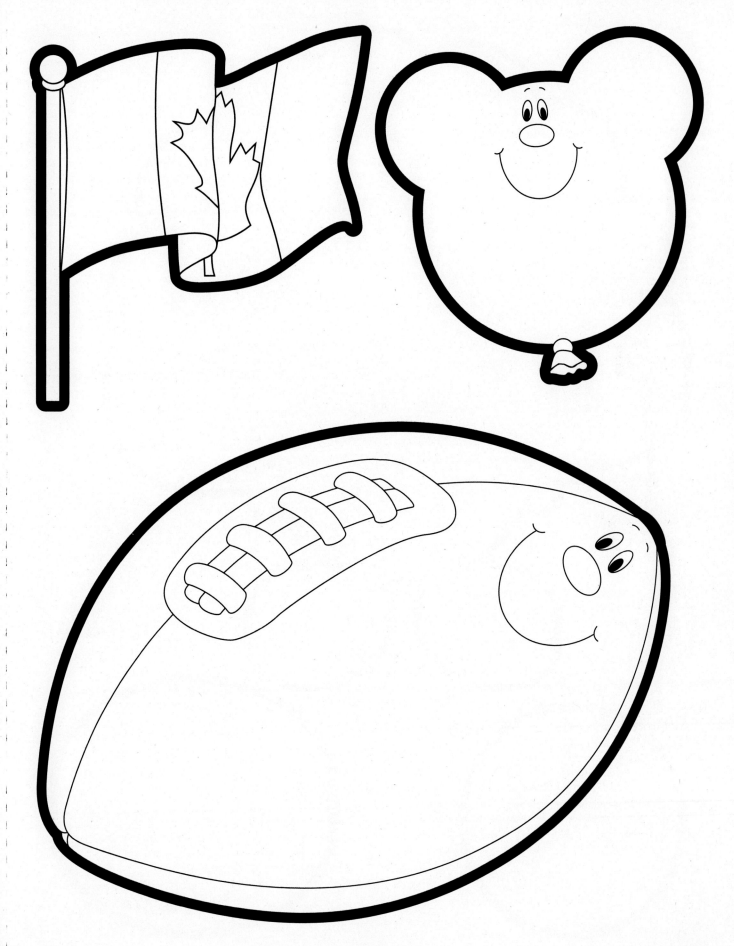

121

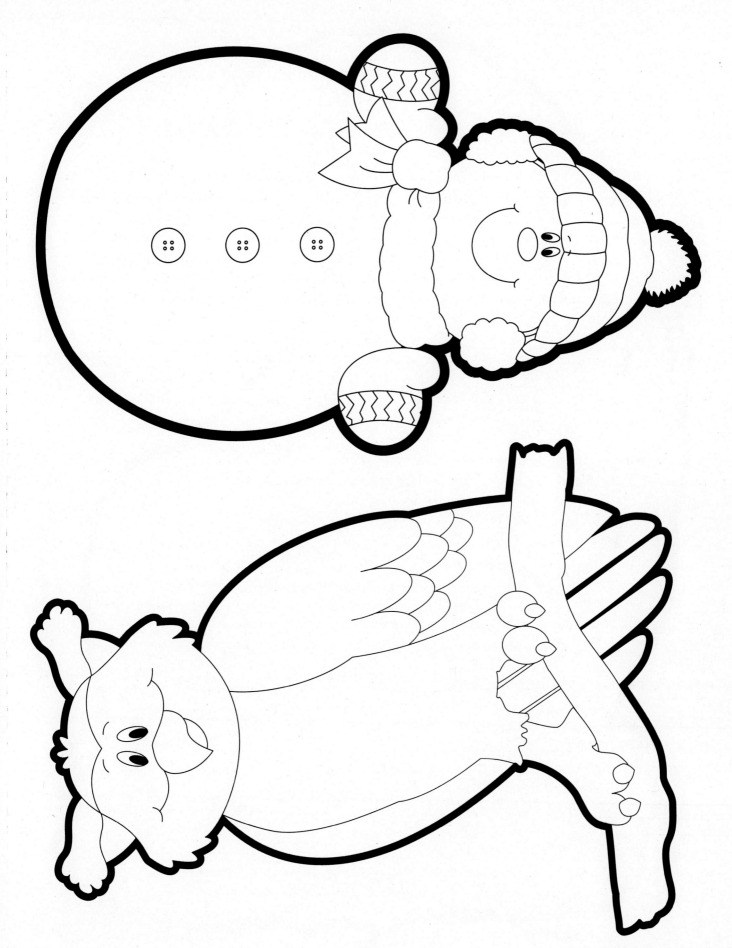

124

126

127